DATE:

PROJECT:

MAIN POINTS:	NOTES:

SUMMARY:

DATE:

PROJECT:

MAIN POINTS:	NOTES:

SUMMARY:

DATE:

PROJECT:

MAIN POINTS:	NOTES:

SUMMARY:

Date:

Project:

Main Points:	Notes:

Summary:

DATE:

PROJECT:

MAIN POINTS:	NOTES:

SUMMARY:

DATE:

PROJECT:

MAIN POINTS:	NOTES:

SUMMARY:

DATE:

PROJECT:

MAIN POINTS:	NOTES:

SUMMARY:

DATE:

PROJECT:

MAIN POINTS:	NOTES:

SUMMARY:

Date:

Project:

Main Points:	Notes:

Summary:

Date:

Project:

Main Points:	Notes:

Summary:

Date:

Project:

Main Points:	Notes:

Summary:

Date:

Project:

Main Points:	Notes:

Summary:

Date:

Project:

Main Points:	Notes:

Summary:

Date:

Project:

Main Points:	Notes:

Summary:

DATE:

PROJECT:

MAIN POINTS:	NOTES:

SUMMARY:

Date:

Project:

Main Points:	Notes:

Summary:

DATE:

PROJECT:

MAIN POINTS:	NOTES:

SUMMARY:

Date:

Project:

Main Points: | **Notes:**

Summary:

DATE:

PROJECT:

MAIN POINTS:	NOTES:

SUMMARY:

DATE:

PROJECT:

MAIN POINTS:	NOTES:

SUMMARY:

Date:

Project:

Main Points:	Notes:

Summary:

DATE:

PROJECT:

MAIN POINTS:	NOTES:

SUMMARY:

DATE:

PROJECT:

MAIN POINTS:	NOTES:

SUMMARY:

DATE:

PROJECT:

MAIN POINTS:	NOTES:

SUMMARY:

Date:

Project:

Main Points:	Notes:

Summary:

Date:

Project:

Main Points:	Notes:

Summary:

Date:

Project:

Main Points:	Notes:

Summary:

DATE:

PROJECT:

MAIN POINTS:	NOTES:

SUMMARY:

DATE:

PROJECT:

MAIN POINTS:	NOTES:

SUMMARY:

Date:

Project:

Main Points:	Notes:

Summary:

Date:

Project:

Main Points:	Notes:

Summary:

Date:

Project:

Main Points:	Notes:

Summary:

Date:

Project:

Main Points:	Notes:

Summary:

Date:

Project:

Main Points:	Notes:

Summary:

DATE:

PROJECT:

MAIN POINTS:	NOTES:

SUMMARY:

Date:

Project:

Main Points:	Notes:

Summary:

Date:

Project:

Main Points: **Notes:**

Summary:

DATE:

PROJECT:

MAIN POINTS:	NOTES:

SUMMARY:

Date:

Project:

Main Points:	Notes:

Summary:

Date:

Project:

Main Points:	Notes:

Summary:

DATE:

PROJECT:

MAIN POINTS:	NOTES:

SUMMARY:

DATE:

PROJECT:

MAIN POINTS:	NOTES:

SUMMARY:

DATE:

PROJECT:

MAIN POINTS:	NOTES:

SUMMARY:

Date:

Project:

Main Points:	Notes:

Summary:

Date:

Project:

Main Points:	Notes:

Summary:

DATE:

PROJECT:

MAIN POINTS:	NOTES:

SUMMARY:

DATE:

PROJECT:

MAIN POINTS:	NOTES:

SUMMARY:

DATE:

PROJECT:

MAIN POINTS:	NOTES:

SUMMARY:

Date:

Project:

Main Points:	Notes:

Summary:

DATE:

PROJECT:

MAIN POINTS:	NOTES:

SUMMARY:

Date:

Project:

Main Points:	Notes:

Summary:

Date:

Project:

Main Points:	Notes:

Summary:

DATE:

PROJECT:

MAIN POINTS:	NOTES:

SUMMARY:

Date:

Project:

Main Points:	Notes:

Summary:

DATE:

PROJECT:

MAIN POINTS:	NOTES:

SUMMARY:

Date:

Project:

Main Points:	Notes:

Summary:

Date:

Project:

Main Points:	Notes:

Summary:

DATE:

PROJECT:

MAIN POINTS:	NOTES:

SUMMARY:

Date:

Project:

Main Points:	Notes:

Summary:

DATE:

PROJECT:

MAIN POINTS:	NOTES:

SUMMARY:

DATE:

PROJECT:

MAIN POINTS:	NOTES:

SUMMARY:

DATE:

PROJECT:

MAIN POINTS:	NOTES:

SUMMARY:

DATE:

PROJECT:

MAIN POINTS:	NOTES:

SUMMARY:

DATE:

PROJECT:

MAIN POINTS:	NOTES:

SUMMARY:

Date:

Project:

Main Points:	Notes:

Summary:

DATE:

PROJECT:

MAIN POINTS:	NOTES:

SUMMARY:

DATE:

PROJECT:

MAIN POINTS:	NOTES:

SUMMARY:

Date:

Project:

Main Points:	Notes:

Summary:

Date:

Project:

Main Points:	Notes:

Summary:

DATE:

PROJECT:

MAIN POINTS:	NOTES:

SUMMARY:

DATE:

PROJECT:

MAIN POINTS:	NOTES:

SUMMARY:

DATE:

PROJECT:

MAIN POINTS:	NOTES:

SUMMARY:

DATE:

PROJECT:

MAIN POINTS:	NOTES:

SUMMARY:

Date:

Project:

Main Points:	Notes:

Summary:

DATE:

PROJECT:

MAIN POINTS:	NOTES:

SUMMARY:

DATE:

PROJECT:

MAIN POINTS:	NOTES:

SUMMARY:

DATE:

PROJECT:

MAIN POINTS:	NOTES:

SUMMARY:

DATE:

PROJECT:

MAIN POINTS:	NOTES:

SUMMARY:

Date:

Project:

Main Points:	Notes:

Summary:

DATE:

PROJECT:

MAIN POINTS:	NOTES:

SUMMARY:

DATE:

PROJECT:

MAIN POINTS:	NOTES:

SUMMARY:

DATE:

PROJECT:

MAIN POINTS:	NOTES:

SUMMARY:

DATE:

PROJECT:

MAIN POINTS:	NOTES:

SUMMARY:

Date:

Project:

Main Points:	Notes:

Summary:

Date:

Project:

Main Points:	Notes:

Summary:

Date:

Project:

Main Points:	Notes:

Summary:

DATE:

PROJECT:

MAIN POINTS:	NOTES:

SUMMARY:

Date:

Project:

Main Points:	Notes:

Summary:

Date:

Project:

Main Points:	Notes:

Summary:

DATE:

PROJECT:

MAIN POINTS:	NOTES:

SUMMARY:

DATE:

PROJECT:

MAIN POINTS:	NOTES:

SUMMARY:

Date:

Project:

Main Points:	Notes:

Summary:

DATE:

PROJECT:

MAIN POINTS:	NOTES:

SUMMARY:

Date:

Project:

Main Points:	Notes:

Summary:

DATE:

PROJECT:

MAIN POINTS:	NOTES:

SUMMARY:

Date:

Project:

Main Points:	Notes:

Summary:

DATE:

PROJECT:

MAIN POINTS:	NOTES:

SUMMARY:

Date:

Project:

Main Points:	Notes:

Summary:

DATE:

PROJECT:

MAIN POINTS:	NOTES:

SUMMARY:

Date:

Project:

Main Points:	Notes:

Summary:

DATE:

PROJECT:

MAIN POINTS:	NOTES:

SUMMARY:

DATE:

PROJECT:

MAIN POINTS:	NOTES:

SUMMARY:

DATE:

PROJECT:

MAIN POINTS:	NOTES:

SUMMARY:

Date:

Project:

Main Points:	Notes:

Summary:

DATE:

PROJECT:

MAIN POINTS:	NOTES:

SUMMARY:

DATE:

PROJECT:

MAIN POINTS:	NOTES:

SUMMARY:

DATE:

PROJECT:

MAIN POINTS:	NOTES:

SUMMARY:

DATE:

PROJECT:

MAIN POINTS:	NOTES:

SUMMARY:

DATE:

PROJECT:

MAIN POINTS:	NOTES:

SUMMARY:

DATE:

PROJECT:

MAIN POINTS:	NOTES:

SUMMARY:

DATE:

PROJECT:

MAIN POINTS:	NOTES:

SUMMARY:

Date:

Project:

Main Points:	Notes:

Summary:

DATE:

PROJECT:

MAIN POINTS:	NOTES:

SUMMARY:

DATE:

PROJECT:

MAIN POINTS:	NOTES:

SUMMARY:

Date:

Project:

Main Points:	Notes:

Summary:

Date:

Project:

Main Points:	Notes:

Summary:

DATE:

PROJECT:

MAIN POINTS:	NOTES:

SUMMARY:

DATE:

PROJECT:

MAIN POINTS:	NOTES:

SUMMARY:

DATE:

PROJECT:

MAIN POINTS:	NOTES:

SUMMARY:

DATE:

PROJECT:

MAIN POINTS:	NOTES:

SUMMARY:

DATE:

PROJECT:

MAIN POINTS:	NOTES:

SUMMARY:

Date:

Project:

Main Points:	Notes:

Summary:

Date:

Project:

Main Points:	Notes:

Summary:

DATE:

PROJECT:

MAIN POINTS:	NOTES:

SUMMARY:

DATE:

PROJECT:

MAIN POINTS:	NOTES:

SUMMARY:

DATE:

PROJECT:

MAIN POINTS:	NOTES:

SUMMARY:

DATE:

PROJECT:

MAIN POINTS:	NOTES:

SUMMARY:

Date:

Project:

Main Points:	Notes:

Summary:

DATE:

PROJECT:

MAIN POINTS:	NOTES:

SUMMARY:

DATE:

PROJECT:

MAIN POINTS:	NOTES:

SUMMARY:

Date:

Project:

Main Points:	Notes:

Summary:

DATE:

PROJECT:

MAIN POINTS:	NOTES:

SUMMARY:

DATE:

PROJECT:

MAIN POINTS:	NOTES:

SUMMARY:

Date:

Project:

Main Points:	Notes:

Summary:

Date:

Project:

Main Points:	Notes:

Summary:

DATE:

PROJECT:

MAIN POINTS:	NOTES:

SUMMARY:

DATE:

PROJECT:

MAIN POINTS:	NOTES:

SUMMARY:

DATE:

PROJECT:

MAIN POINTS:	NOTES:

SUMMARY:

DATE:

PROJECT:

MAIN POINTS:	NOTES:

SUMMARY:

DATE:

PROJECT:

MAIN POINTS:	NOTES:

SUMMARY:

DATE:

PROJECT:

MAIN POINTS:	NOTES:

SUMMARY:

DATE:

PROJECT:

MAIN POINTS:	NOTES:

SUMMARY:

DATE:

PROJECT:

MAIN POINTS:	NOTES:

SUMMARY:

DATE:

PROJECT:

MAIN POINTS:	NOTES:

SUMMARY:

DATE:

PROJECT:

MAIN POINTS:	NOTES:

SUMMARY:

DATE:

PROJECT:

MAIN POINTS:	NOTES:

SUMMARY:

DATE:

PROJECT:

MAIN POINTS:	NOTES:

SUMMARY:

DATE:

PROJECT:

MAIN POINTS:	NOTES:

SUMMARY:

DATE:

PROJECT:

MAIN POINTS:	NOTES:

SUMMARY:

Date:

Project:

Main Points:	Notes:

Summary:

DATE:

PROJECT:

MAIN POINTS:	NOTES:

SUMMARY:

DATE:

PROJECT:

MAIN POINTS:	NOTES:

SUMMARY:

DATE:

PROJECT:

MAIN POINTS:	NOTES:

SUMMARY:

Date:

Project:

Main Points:	Notes:

Summary:

DATE:

PROJECT:

MAIN POINTS:	NOTES:

SUMMARY:

Date:

Project:

Main Points:	Notes:

Summary:

DATE:

PROJECT:

MAIN POINTS:	NOTES:

SUMMARY:

Date:

Project:

Main Points:	Notes:

Summary:

DATE:

PROJECT:

MAIN POINTS:	NOTES:

SUMMARY:

DATE:

PROJECT:

MAIN POINTS:	NOTES:

SUMMARY:

Date:

Project:

Main Points:	Notes:

Summary: